CLOTHES OF THE MODERN WORLD

CHRISTINE HATT

Illustrated by DANUTA MAYER

PETER BEDRICK BOOKS

This American edition published 2002 by
Peter Bedrick Books, an imprint of
McGraw-Hill Children's Publishing,
8787 Orion Place, Columbus, Ohio 43240

First published in the UK in 2001 by
Belitha Press Limited, London House,
Great Eastern Wharf, Parkgate Road,
London SW11 4NQ

Library of Congress Cataloging-in-Publication Data
Hatt, Christine.
   Clothes of the modern world / Christine Hatt ; illustrated by Danuta Mayer.
      p.cm. -- (Dress sense)
   Includes index.
   ISBN 0-87226-667-2
   1.Costume--History--20th century--Juvenile literature. 2. Costume--History--19th
century--Juvenile literature. [1.Costume--History. 2. Clothing and dress--History.] I.
Mayer, Danuta. II. Title. III. Series.

GT596 .H38 2001
391--dc21   2001025259

Series editor: Claire Edwards
Series designer: Angie Allison
US Editor: Teresa Domnauer
Editor: Jinny Johnson
Illustrator: Danuta Mayer
Picture researcher: Diana Morris
Consultant: Dr Jane Bridgeman
Education consultant: Anne Washtell

Printed in China
10 9 8 7 6 5 4 3 2 1

EAN

9 780872 266674

McGraw-Hill
Children's Publishing
A Division of The McGraw-Hill Companies

Picture acknowledgements:
Dr Jane Bridgeman: 7tl
Sipa/Rex Features: 7br
Eileen Tweedy/Tate Gallery London/The Art Archive:
6br
Victoria & Albert Museum/The Art Archive: 6tl

The cover illustration shows three styles
of women's dress from the Modern era.
The woman on the left is wearing a *haute
couture* dress by Yves Saint-Laurent, with a
pattern based on a painting by Dutch artist
Piet Mondrian (see page 31). The woman in
the middle wears a mini-dress created by top
French designer André Courrèges in 1967, and
the woman on the right a simple shift dress
created by the Jean Muir design house in 2000
(see page 35).

The illustration below shows the Artificial
Silk Exhibition of 1926 (see page 41).

CONTENTS

Words in **bold** are explained in the glossary.

INTRODUCTION

This book shows you what people from many countries have worn since 1800. That year marked the approximate end of the **Early Modern era** of history, following the formation of the U.S.A. and the **French Revolution**. It also marked the beginning of the Modern era, which continues today.

This 1862 outfit is typical of the elaborate clothing worn by women in Victorian Britain.

This Victorian man has dared to wear a low-crowned hat, not a top hat, with his formal outfit.

Changing fashions

Fashions have altered greatly in modern times. The development of women's clothing has reflected women's changing role. For example, in the mid-nineteenth century, when rich women spent most of their lives at home, they wore huge **crinolines** and tight corsets that limited their movements. Today, when many women go out to work and play sports, short skirts and pants allow them to move freely. Men's clothes have also become more informal. For example, in the late nineteenth century men began to wear **lounge suits** instead of formal clothing.

Industrialization

The way in which clothes are made has also changed dramatically over the last 200 years. For example **power looms**, first built during the **Industrial Revolution**, allowed people to weave fabric more quickly than ever before (see pages 40–41). Sewing machines, invented in 1846, made it possible to mass-produce **ready-to-wear** garments. New, **synthetic** fabrics have also altered the clothing industry. Scientists produced the first, including **nylon**, during the mid-1900s (see page 25).

In the twenty-first century, women dress for comfort and ease of movement.

Today, many men wear simple, two-piece lounge suits like this for work.

A suit created by famous designer Mary Quant (see pages 30–31) in 1962.

Twentieth-century developments

Many other changes affected clothing in the twentieth century. People began to copy the dress of film, TV, and pop stars, and from the 1950s, teenagers developed their own styles. The fashion industry altered, too. From the 1960s, top designers concentrated on affordable ready-to-wear clothes rather than costly *haute couture*, and created a range of styles rather than one 'look' each season. Now, in the twenty-first century, fashion changes faster and is more fascinating than ever.

About this book

The next two pages show you how experts know what people wore in the past and how they keep track of modern fashions. Each double page that follows describes the clothing of a particular place and time. Material Matters boxes give more information on types of material from which clothes were made. Other boxes give information on special subjects such as uniforms. There is a brief timeline at the top of each page, and maps on pages 44–45 show many of the places mentioned.

A Mary Quant dress of 1966, with a mini-skirt that finishes at mid-thigh.

The West and the World

As contact between the West—Europe and the Americas—and the rest of the world has increased through travel and communications, Western fashions have spread around the globe. Now businessmen almost everywhere dress in suits and ties, and women wear styles copied from the catwalks of London, Paris, Milan, or New York. Despite this trend, many communities have kept their traditional costume (see pages 36–39). Even in Westernized countries, people wear national clothing for special occasions. In Japan, for example, quilted robes, **kimonos**, and **obi** sashes are often worn at festivals and weddings (see left).

HOW WE KNOW

Historians who study the costume of the last two centuries can gain information from a variety of sources. Like experts who study the dress of earlier eras, they examine surviving garments and illustrations. They read books that contain costume descriptions, too. But they can also look at photographs and films, two great inventions of the nineteenth century.

This luxurious nightgown and negligee were made in 1922. They are part of the costume collection at London's Victoria and Albert Museum.

Surviving garments

Thousands of clothing items made in modern times have survived. Many are displayed in important museums, such as the Fashion and Textile Museum in Paris and the Victoria and Albert Museum in London. The Costume Institute in New York's Metropolitan Museum of Art owns 60,000 garments and accessories. Fashion houses and private collectors, as well as rich and royal families, have also preserved costumes of this era.

Evidence from art

Artists of the nineteenth and twentieth centuries often painted costumes in detail, so their work gives useful evidence for experts. For example, French-born painter James Tissot drew the men and women of Victorian England in close-up. The Frenchman Jean Ingres created portraits of French beauties in all their finery. In the U.S.A., George Bellows painted both portraits of the glamorous rich and city scenes showing the poor.

This James Tissot picture, *The Ball on Shipboard*, was painted in 1874. It clearly shows dresses with tight **bodices** and full skirts draped over **bustles**. These were the height of fashion at the time.

Fashion plates

In the nineteenth century, fashion plates (illustrations of the latest fashions) appeared in magazines such as *La Belle Assemblée*, published in London, *Godey's Lady's Book,*

This cover from a 1920s' issue of the magazine *Les Modes* features a hand-colored photograph. It shows a young woman wearing a low-waisted dress, heeled **court shoes**, and a straw hat.

published in Philadelphia, and *Le Journal des dames et des modes*, published in Paris. In the twentieth century, they were featured in journals such as *Vogue*. Many plates, such as those by French illustrator Horace Vernet, can still be studied today.

By the book

Novels often contain useful descriptions of costume, but other types of books are also helpful to historians. Nineteenth-century guides to correct behavior often told readers what to wear. For example, *The Habits of Good Society*, published in England, gave details of the four types of fashionable men's coats. Manuals written for tailors in England, France, and many other countries are also full of information.

Fashion photography

Fashion photography became important at the start of the twentieth century. *Les Modes*, a French magazine also sold in London and New York, was among the first magazines to publish clothing photographs. One of the best early fashion photographers was an American called Man Ray, who worked for fashion magazines such as *Vogue*. Fashion photographs still appear in magazines, allowing experts and the public to follow the latest fashion trends.

Fashion on Film

The film industry grew up in the early twentieth century. By the 1920s studios in Hollywood and elsewhere were thriving. Outfits worn by actors, from the slinky dresses of 1930s' star Greta Garbo to the T-shirts and leather jackets of 1950s' heart-throb James Dean (see right), are captured forever on film, so experts can see them again and again.

EARLY NINETEENTH-CENTURY FRANCE

From about 1830, some women wore a see-through cape called a **canezou** over their dresses.

During the French Revolution, from 1789 to 1799, the monarchy was overthrown and elaborate court dress went out of fashion. It returned after 1804, when Napoleon I began to rule France as emperor. But the simple revolutionary styles were not entirely abandoned.

Women's fashions

Women in Napoleon's 'First Empire' still wore dresses of a late eighteenth-century style, which were loosely based on ancient Greek fashions. These **Empire line** garments had low necklines, high waistlines, and often short, puffed sleeves. Eighteenth-century dresses had been made of flimsy fabrics such as **muslin**, but in the nineteenth century **linen** and **calico** were more popular. Court dresses were made of velvet, silk, or satin and had trains.

Changing styles

Napoleon's rule came to an end in 1814 and the monarchy was restored. By then women's dress was changing, and this trend continued. The waistline returned to its normal place and skirts flared out in a bell shape. **Leg-of-mutton sleeves** (see far right) became common. For modesty, low necklines were covered with a scarf called a *fichu* or filled with another piece of fabric.

Menswear

Frenchmen of the early nineteenth century admired the skill of London tailors, so followed English fashions. They wore four main garments—a **tailcoat**, britches or pants, a waistcoat, and a shirt. Shirts had high collars and were worn with a **cravat** or **stock** at the neck. From the 1820s, **frock coats** replaced tail coats for daywear and britches gradually went out of fashion.

Napoleon I in his uniform of leather boots, white britches, waistcoat, and decorated tailcoat.

A type of overcoat called a carrick, which had several capes under the collar, became popular in this era.

Two types of men's coats. On the left is a **cutaway tailcoat**. On the right is a tight-waisted frock coat.

1804	1813	1814	1815	1821
Napoleon crowns himself Emperor of France.	Napoleon's troops defeated at Leipzig.	Napoleon abdicates and is banished to the island of Elba.	Napoleon returns but is defeated at Battle of Waterloo and exiled to St. Helena.	Death of Napoleon.

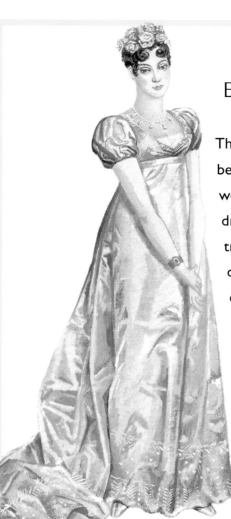

TWO WOMEN EARLY NINETEENTH CENTURY

The woman on the left is Marie Louise, who in 1809 became the second wife of Napoleon I. She is wearing typical court costume of the time. Her dress has a high waist, short sleeves, and a long train, and is made from ice-blue satin with a decorated border. A pearl necklace and a headdress of pink flowers complete her outfit.

The woman on the right is wearing an 1830s' dress. It has leg-of-mutton sleeves and a low neckline filled with lace. The waist is in its natural place, and a buckled belt emphasizes its narrowness. It was necessary to wear a corset to achieve this shape. The woman also wears a feathered bonnet and short, tight boots.

Medieval Modes

In the early nineteenth century, the Romantic movement in art, literature, and music swept across Europe. It was concerned not with the order of science and religion, but with strong human feelings, nature, and the supernatural. Many Romantic novels, such as *The Hunch-Back of Notre-Dame* by Victor Hugo, were set in the Middle Ages. As a result, some women began to wear mock medieval clothes. **Renaissance** fashions, such as slashed sleeves (see right), also became highly popular.

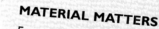

MATERIAL MATTERS

France's textile industry almost collapsed during the Revolution. Napoleon set out to improve the situation, but his wars with other countries made it difficult for manufacturers to sell their goods and make a profit. Despite these problems, high-quality fabrics were produced in France during this era. The Jouy factory near Paris was famous for its brightly colored, printed cottons. So, too, were factories in the northeastern region of Alsace. Typical materials from this area were dyed a shade of bright red, known as Turkey red (see left).

LATE NINETEENTH-CENTURY FRANCE

In 1852, Napoleon III, nephew of Napoleon I, became Emperor of France and the Second Empire began. Napoleon and his wife, Eugénie, introduced an era of great elegance. Paris, the French capital, was partly rebuilt and the rich dressed in finery to visit its new opera house and parks. Now French fashions led the world.

This 1870s' bustle is made of horsehair. 1880s' bustles were often made of wire.

This woman wears a whalebone corset and a cage crinoline over a plain cotton **chemise** and **drawers**.

The age of the crinoline

By the late 1830s, dress skirts had grown very wide, curving out in a great sweep from the waist. To create this shape, women had to wear many wool or cotton petticoats. In the 1840s, they also began to wear horsehair petticoats, the first **crinolines**, for extra width. Then, in the 1850s, a French designer invented a framework of steel hoops called a **cage crinoline**. Worn under skirts, these crinolines produced the fashionable shape without the need for so many hot, heavy petticoats.

The morning coat had tapered sides and rounded tails at the back.

Changing shapes

Crinolines slowly grew wider and by 1860 hems measured up to 33 feet. From the mid-1860s, the full crinoline was replaced by the flat-fronted half-crinoline, then the horsehair **bustle**, over which many folds of fabric were draped. The bustle disappeared in the late 1870s, but grew popular again in the 1880s.

Coats and suits

Men's clothing changed little during the late nineteenth century. The **morning coat** (see right) became a popular item of daywear. Also, shorter, informal jackets were introduced from England. From the 1870s, the jackets were often worn with matching pants and waistcoats to form suits. Fabric colors gradually became darker.

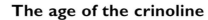

Accessories for a night at the opera—a man's opera hat, which could be squashed flat and stowed under the seat, a woman's fan, and opera glasses.

From the 1870s, elegant Frenchwomen liked to wear satin mules with small heels.

1871
Revolutionary Commune
government briefly rules Paris.

1889
World Exhibition held in Paris
to celebrate the French Empire.

1889
Eiffel Tower built in Paris to mark
the centenary of the French Revolution.

MATERIAL MATTERS

Encouraged by Napoleon III and his wife, Eugénie, craftsmen in the French city of Lyon made all sorts of fine silks during the Second Empire, including high-quality silk velvets. They used the latest Jacquard looms (see pages 40-41) to work a wide variety of patterns into the weave. But the Empress Eugénie herself preferred plain silks, so these became the most fashionable.

The Birth of *Haute Couture*

Until the 1850s, all rich women had their clothes made by dressmakers, who visited them at home. Then, in 1857, Englishman Charles Frederick Worth set up a fashion house in central Paris. By designing beautiful, well-cut clothes and employing women to model them in his salon, he soon attracted important customers from all over the world. They included the Empress Eugénie herself. In this way, **haute couture**—the designer-led, high-fashion business—was born.

SKIRT STYLES 1870S AND 1880S

The woman on the left is wearing an evening gown of the late 1870s. The tight bodice, worn over a corset, has short sleeves and a low neck. The striped overskirt is pulled up to reveal a plain underskirt. There is no bustle, but the mass of material at the back is gathered in with artificial flowers. The dress ends in a long train typical of the era.

The woman on the right wears a skirt and jacket of the late 1880s. By this time, the bustle had returned to fashion. Now it was usually made of stiff wire and larger than the earlier horsehair versions. As a result, skirts stuck straight out from the waist at the back. The woman has completed her outfit with a flower-decorated hat and a parasol.

11

EARLY NINETEENTH-CENTURY BRITAIN

This 1814 dress features the frills and gathers typical of the period in Britain.

Two ways of tying cravats. The loose bow (top) was known as the Byron style after poet George Byron.

British men, and especially a man called Beau Brummell (see box), led the male fashion world in the early nineteenth century. But women's fashion followed trends set in the French capital, Paris.

Female fashions

At the end of the eighteenth century, the simple, high-waisted gowns worn in France were also common in Britain. But from 1799 the two countries were at war, and fashion news rarely reached London from Paris. So British styles began to develop separately, influenced by the Romantic movement (see page 9). Dresses were decorated with fancy ribbons and frills. The novels of Scottish writer Sir Walter Scott made tartan popular, too. When the wars ended in 1815, British women rushed to Paris and again became followers of French fashion.

Spencers and shawls

Some women's garments worn in Britain during the early nineteenth century were copied in France. They included the spencer, introduced in the 1790s. This was a tight, short jacket, generally in a bright color and worn over a white dress. Another was the shawl made of cashmere (see far right) or other materials such as **muslin**.

Menswear

At the beginning of the century, many British men wore plain **cutaway tailcoats** (see page 8), patterned waistcoats and knee britches or, sometimes, pants. As in France, coat types changed over the following years. Waisted **frock coats** were common from the 1820s. Pants became more popular and were often striped. By the 1830s, britches had died out, and dark fabrics were beginning to replace light and brightly colored materials.

This woman wears a silk spencer and dress and holds a drawstring bag called a reticule.

This style of leather military boot was named after the Duke of Wellington. He led Britain to victory in the 1815 Battle of Waterloo.

1811–1820
Regency Period: the future King George IV
(the Prince Regent) rules on behalf of his sick father.

1815
British defeat Napoleon and his
troops at the Battle of Waterloo.

1820–1830
Reign of King George IV.

A COUNTRYMAN AND A KING
1810 AND 1820

The man on the left is a typical English country
gentleman of the early nineteenth century. He is wearing
the standard garments of the period—**cutaway tailcoat**, waistcoat, shirt, and britches. All are simply
cut and made of plain woolen cloth without any
trimmings. A black top hat and sturdy wooden
walking stick complete the man's outfit.

The man on the right is George IV (see
below), who was king from 1820 to 1830. His
outer garment is a frock coat trimmed with fur and
braid. On his legs he wears britches and silk socks,
and on his feet are low-heeled shoes called pumps.
These were common items of court and evening dress
in the early nineteenth century.

Dashing Dandies

1811 to 1820 is known as the Regency
Period in Britain, because during that
time the country was ruled by the Prince
Regent, later King George IV. He loved fine
clothes and gathered well-dressed friends
around him. Among them was Beau
Brummell, whose stylish coats and
buckskin pants always fitted perfectly.
Brummell was a dandy—a man with a
great, perhaps too great, interest in
fashion. However, his style was simple. Later dandies
preferred more extreme fashions, such as high
collars, padded chests, and tiny waists (see above).

MATERIAL MATTERS

The fashionable shawls of this period originally
came from Kashmir, then part of India. Made of
cashmere, a type of soft goats' wool, they often
had a pattern of ovals with curved tips, known
as Kashmir cones. In the nineteenth century,
the French and British
began to make similar
shawls. Most British
shawls were made in
Paisley, near Glasgow
in Scotland. As a
result, materials with
a cone pattern are
known as Paisley
fabrics (see left).

13

LATE NINETEENTH-CENTURY BRITAIN

Queen Victoria ruled Britain from 1837 to 1901. In her reign, the country became a world power with an empire abroad and strong industries at home. Victorian men wore dark clothing in order to look serious and important. Women dressed in French styles, but with British variations. They aimed to appear feminine and modest.

Victorian girls wore short crinolines, showing their frilly pantalettes (**drawers**).

Style changes

Throughout Victorian times, men continued to wear dress pants, coats, and waistcoats. However, there were some changes. The **morning coat** (see page 10) became common, and also the sack coat (see left), often worn with striped pants and a bowler hat. The **Chesterfield** was a popular type of overcoat from the 1840s.

A rich Victorian gentleman of the 1850s in a **frock coat** and slacks (above).

Sack coats were for informal occasions only. Their edges were often trimmed with braid.

Crinolines and capes

By the 1840s, women's dresses had waists in their natural position, bell-shaped skirts and tight bodices, often with close-fitting sleeves. In the 1850s, the **cage crinoline** was enthusiastically adopted in Britain, but it did have some opponents (see right). The dresses worn over the top varied in style—different types were worn indoors and outdoors, and in the morning, afternoon, and evening.

Princess gowns

As in France (see pages 10–11), the cage crinoline went out of fashion in the 1860s, to be replaced by the **bustle**. One popular style worn over bustles was the princess gown. It had a bodice and skirt made from one piece of material and fitted the body closely. This required a new, longer corset. One elaborate type of princess gown was named the Dolly Varden (see right), after a character from the novels of Charles Dickens.

A princess gown made of plain fabric. The more ornate Dolly Varden style had patterned fabric.

This is a chatelaine—a type of chain Victorian women attached to their waists and on which they hung keys and other items.

MATERIAL MATTERS

Until modern times, materials were dyed using natural substances taken from plants, insects, and shellfish. Then, in 1856, British chemist William Henry Perkin created the first **synthetic** dye. It produced a purple color and was given the name "mauve," the French word for the pinkish-purple mallow flower. Soon, many more synthetic dyes were created and used to color fabric. Some people loved them, but others thought that the colors were too bright and artificial.

The Rational Dress Society

Some British writers and artists disapproved of late nineteenth-century costume, which they thought was ugly and uncomfortable. They believed that clothes should be loose and not force the body into unnatural shapes with corsets and lacing. So they formed the Rational Dress Society and wore garments that they considered acceptable. Women wore flowing robes without corsets, and flat shoes. Men wore britches or pants and smoking jackets.

DAY AND NIGHT 1860s

The woman on the left is dressed in an evening gown of the late 1860s. It is worn over a half-crinoline, so the skirt sticks out much more at the back than at the front. The gown bodice has short sleeves and a low neck. Despite the Victorian fashion for modesty, this was a common evening-wear style.

The two women on the right are dressed for daytime in the full crinolines of the early 1860s. One wears a flounced purple dress decorated with bows. The other wears a brown dress with a special type of three-quarter-length coat called a casaque on the top. Both also have bonnets tied with large bows under the chin.

NINETEENTH-CENTURY U.S.A.

The nineteenth century was a time of great change in the U.S.A. Immigrants poured in from all over the world. New York and other Northern cities grew rapidly. In the South, huge farms and cotton plantations flourished. Meanwhile, the country was expanding steadily west (see pages 18–19). The costumes of the rich were mainly based on European styles, but there were some distinctively American trends, too.

Clothes-making became the biggest industry in New York in the 1800s.

This American woman of 1830 wears a long-sleeved, Empire line gown with a lace-trimmed neckline.

Spreading the word

Magazines brought news of women's fashions worn in London and Paris to the U.S.A. Early publications, such as *Godey's Lady's Book*, contained redrawn, often inaccurate versions of European fashion plates. But later magazines such as *Harper's Bazaar*, founded in 1867, printed copies of the original drawings. Rich American women also went to Europe to buy clothes. So, as in Europe, **Empire line** gowns, then styles based on **crinolines** and **bustles**, were all popular for a time in the U.S.A.

Amelia Bloomer

Not everyone in the U.S.A. approved of heavy crinolines and bustles. Amelia Bloomer thought that women should wear more practical clothes and so promoted the Bloomer costume (see far right). A few American women wore this outfit, but in general it was unpopular.

American glassmaker Louis Comfort Tiffany made beautiful jewelry. This iris-shaped brooch dates from about 1900.

East and West

Wealthy American men who lived in the East of the country usually followed European fashions, although sometimes they were a few months behind the latest trends. But in the West, new garments suitable for a quite different way of life gradually emerged (see pages 18–19).

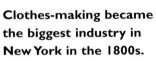

Nineteenth-century U.S. presidents such as John Quincy Adams (above) wore European-style clothing.

1865
13th Amendment to the constitution ends slavery in the U.S.A.

1865–1877
The Reconstruction era; U.S.A. is reunited and rebuilt after the Civil War.

1867
Harper's Bazaar magazine founded.

SHORT AND LONG 1850S AND 1860S

The woman on the left is Amelia Bloomer, who is wearing the Bloomer costume. It is made up of three main items—a long, fringed bodice, a short skirt that finishes just below the knee and a pair of baggy pants. This style of pants became known as "bloomers" after their inventor.

The picture on the right is based on a *Harper's Bazaar* fashion plate of 1869. It shows a woman in a ***polonaise*** gown, with an overskirt pulled up over an underskirt. She also wears a ***fichu*** scarf. The *polonaise* was made popular by eighteenth-century French queen Marie Antoinette. In the nineteenth century, it was worn by Empress Eugénie (see pages 10–11), who was admired and copied by American women.

The Civil War

In 1861, the northern and southern states of the U.S.A. began a civil war. There were several reasons for the conflict, but in particular, the South supported slavery, while the North did not. During the war, the Confederate soldiers, from the South (bottom right), wore grey uniforms. The Union soldiers, from the North (top right), wore blue. The North won the war in 1865.

MATERIAL MATTERS

By the mid-nineteenth century, Georgia, Alabama, and other southern states of the U.S.A. produced 75 percent of the world's raw cotton. It was grown on plantations by harshly treated black slaves. Much of the cotton was exported to Britain, where it was turned into cloth in factories. The U.S.A. had set up textile factories later than Britain, but by the 1850s some were producing printed cottons. Many more factories were established after the Civil War. The cottons were first used for garments, but when these wore out, they were often recycled into quilts.

THE AMERICAN WEST

Here, Davy Crockett wears the typical frontiersman's clothes of buckskin tunic, pants, and moccasins.

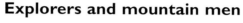

When the U.S.A. was founded in the eighteenth century, it was a strip of land along North America's east coast. But during the nineteenth century, the country took over French, Spanish, and Mexican **colonies** to the west. By mid-century, thousands of immigrants were crossing the continent to places such as California.

People who crossed America in wagons took sturdy, simple clothes. These girls wear printed cotton dresses, while the boy has denim dungarees.

Explorers and mountain men

The first Americans to move west were not ordinary families, but explorers and adventurers, who dressed in rough clothes made of animal skins. Many also wore **moccasins** and raccoon-fur hats. Mountain men who trapped beavers in the Rocky Mountains dressed in a similar way. Some married American Indian women, who knew how to clean, tan, and make clothes from skins.

California was first a Spanish, then a Mexican colony, so its people had distinctive clothing.

Traveling dress

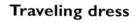

Families made the westward trek in wagons and packed hard-wearing clothes for the journey. Women usually took several full-length dresses, either waisted or loose. Some were lightweight wool dresses called delaines, while others were made of printed cotton. Men dressed in simple wool or cotton shirts and **linsey-woolsey** trousers.

Dressed for the West

Once they had reached the West, settlers made cloth by spinning and weaving **flax**, wool, and cotton, then sewed it into garments. As towns grew up, it became possible to buy fabric and clothes in shops. But the shops rarely sold the fine fashions available on the East coast. Then, in 1872, mail-order companies began to operate in the West and it became easier to dress in the latest styles.

This gold miner of the 1849 Gold Rush is wearing a shirt decorated with picks and shovels. These were the tools of his trade.

1853
Gadsden Purchase completes U.S. land gains in the West.

1866–1886
The era of the cowboy and the "Cattle Kingdom" in the West.

1867
Peace Commission declares that American Indians must leave their lands and live on reservations.

MATERIAL MATTERS

The first jeans were produced in 1850 by San Francisco tailor Levi Strauss. They were made of brown canvas and designed for use by gold miners. Cowboys also adopted these hard-wearing garments, which were soon being made from denim instead. This heavy blue cotton fabric originally came from Nîmes in France—de Nîmes (denim) is French for 'from Nîmes'.

American Indians

The American Indians, who were the original inhabitants of the Great Plains, wore animal skin tunics and leggings. During the nineteenth century, the people were forced off their lands by European settlers. As their lives changed, so did their clothes. For example, they began to decorate garments with new designs, often made from imported glass beads. On this shirt, images of a hand—the ancient American Indian symbol of a warrior—are combined with pictures of the U.S. flag.

COLORFUL COWBOYS 1870S

After the Civil War (see page 17), cattle ranches were set up on the Great Plains of North America. Cowboys were hired to look after the animals. These men learned their skills from Mexicans who had worked on Spanish ranches farther south. They also copied the Mexicans' special clothes.

The cowboy on the left wears denim pants and leather boots with spurs. The leather chaps (leggings) over his pants protect his legs from injury and from prickly plants such as cacti. The cowboy on the right wears hair pants—chaps with the fur still on the leather. Both men also have **bandannas**, which they could pull up over their mouths to keep out dust. Stetson hats, made of beaver felt, cover their heads.

EARLY TWENTIETH-CENTURY EUROPE

Women of this era forced their bodies into the fashionable S-shape with firm whalebone corsets.

The years from 1890 to the start of the First World War in 1914 were known in France as the *belle époque* (beautiful period). In this era, rich European aristocrats enjoyed an extravagant lifestyle. They had outfits for every occasion, from grand balls to sporting competitions.

A new outline

Bustles disappeared from women's clothing for good in the 1890s, after making a brief comeback in the 1880s (see pages 10–11). It now became fashionable to wear long, bell-shaped gowns that flared out into a train at the hem. Necklines were high and sleeves either close-fitting or in the **leg-of-mutton** style (see pages 8–9). Tailor-mades (tailored suits) also grew popular.

The S-shape

In 1900, as Britain's Edwardian period was about to start, styles changed again. Women began to wear corsets that pushed the bust forwards and the hips backwards, forcing their bodies into an S-shape. Gowns of this period were elaborately decorated with lace, embroidery, and crochet. Frilly lace blouses were also popular. From about 1908, a more natural outline replaced the S-shape, and in 1914 the first brassières (bras) were produced.

Old and new

Rich men of the pre-war era continued to wear dark pants, waistcoats, and **morning** or **frock coats** on formal occasions. **Lounge suits** with short jackets were acceptable casual wear. The British king Edward VII, who came to the throne in 1901, wore his suit with a Homburg hat (see right). Special coats, caps, and goggles were designed for driving, a new craze that swept Europe.

"Bloomers," pants similar to those designed by Amelia Bloomer (see pages 16–17), became popular cycling wear in the 1890s.

This woman is wearing a blue suit that shows off her S-shape. The aim of women at this time was to look like the "Gibson Girls"—models with perfect figures first drawn by American artist Charles Dana Gibson.

Many British men copied the soft Homburg hats and lounge suits worn by King Edward VII.

War Wear

During the war, many dress designers, including Frenchman Jean Patou, joined the army and stopped producing collections. In any case, most people did not feel they should dress extravagantly while the fighting continued. In Britain, various styles of simple, hard-wearing **utility clothing** were introduced (see right). Women in many countries began to dress in more practical clothes and shoes, because they had to work in factories and on farms while men were away at war. Underwear also became looser so that women could move easily.

MATERIAL MATTERS

From about 1890 to 1910, a style of art and architecture known as **Art Nouveau** became fashionable. It usually featured images of plants and leaves, often arranged in swirling shapes. Art Nouveau designs were woven into many fabrics of the period. This French example, dating from 1900, contains a repeating image of yellow laburnum flowers.

GLORIOUS GOWNS 1908–1914

These women show two of the gown styles that were popular between 1908 and the beginning of the First World War. The woman on the left wears an afternoon dress of kingfisher-blue silk. It is belted at the waist, but not forced into the S-shape of earlier years.

The woman on the right wears a loose gown, tunic, and turban based on a design by Frenchman Paul Poiret. He, like many others, was influenced by costumes of the Ballets Russes, a Russian ballet company that visited Paris in 1909 and London in 1911. The exotic, Oriental shapes and bright colors of the outfits worn by the dancers remained popular until the war. Poiret also designed the hobble skirt, a narrow-hemmed style that made it extremely difficult to walk.

THE 1920S

During the First World War, many European women worked outside the home for the first time (see page 21). When the war ended, many did not want to return to their old ways of life. They wanted to have jobs, vote in elections, and play sports like men. Fashion reflected women's new roles and ideals. Dresses became simpler and straighter, and hair was cut short. Curves and corsets were out, and the slim, boyish look was in.

Dresses designed by Chanel. The dress on the left dates from 1916. The "little black dress" on the right is from 1926.

"Flatteners" were worn to squash the bust and achieve a fashionable slim shape. Suspenders were attached to the corset.

The barrel line

Even before the end of the war, designers such as Frenchwoman Gabrielle "Coco" Chanel were making dresses that were almost straight. After 1918, this barrel line became a major trend. Many dresses either had no waistline or a low waistline at hip level. From 1924, this was the only truly fashionable style. In the same year, hemlines began to creep up, first reaching mid-calf, then rising to the knee. Women wore silk stockings, held up by suspenders, to show off their newly visible legs and ankles.

1920s' women who had the masculine Eton crop hairstyle sometimes also wore men's suits and ties.

Hats and hairstyles

The most fashionable hat of this era was the tight-fitting **cloche**, sometimes with an upturned brim. To wear it successfully, women had to have short, carefully shaped hair. So the **bob** of the early century was replaced by the **shingle**, then by the more severe Eton crop (see left).

The 1920s' man

Men's fashions changed during this era, too, but not as dramatically. The **lounge suit** grew increasingly common, while the **frock coat** died out. New styles included the very wide pants known as Oxford bags. Plus fours, a style of **knickerbockers**, were popular with golfers.

Oxford bags (left) were up to 24 inches wide round the ankles. Plus fours (right) were so called because four inches of fabric hung below the knee.

During this era, women commonly wore T-strap shoes, such as this gold leather pair from 1925.

SHORT AND LONG MID- AND LATE 1920S

The woman on the left is dressed in a typical outfit of the mid-1920s. The long-sleeved velvet dress has an uneven hemline, a low waist, and a V-neck. It is topped with a matching three-quarter length, buttonless jacket with monkey fur on the sleeves and hem. The woman also wears a brimmed cloche hat and a pair of pointed shoes with high heels.

After 1927, fashions changed again and skirts slowly lengthened. Some dresses had short skirts under longer, see-through overskirts, so combining two styles. The green evening dress on the right, created by famous French designer Madeleine Vionnet, was an example of this trend.

MATERIAL MATTERS

All sorts of fabrics were popular during the 1920s, from the everyday to the extremely glamorous. Ordinary wool made a fashion come-back in short-sleeved or sleeveless jumpers. Kasha, a soft and expensive material made from the fleeces of Himalayan sheep, was used in clothing for the first time. Lamé, produced by weaving gold or silver threads into cotton, silk, or wool, was often chosen for glittering evening wear.

Dressed for Dance

Several energetic new dances were invented during the 1920s. They included the Black Bottom and the Charleston, which both came from the U.S.A. Professional dancers wore extremely short, heavily sequinned and beaded dresses (see left) to perform in special competitions and shows. Some ordinary women also dared to step out in these dazzling creations.

1890–1973
Life of Elsa Schiaparelli.

1929
Wall Street Crash takes place in the U.S.A.; the Depression begins and spreads to Europe; millions lose their jobs.

1933
Franklin D. Roosevelt becomes U.S. president and introduces the "New Deal" to combat the Depression.

THE 1930S

Several new trends for women's clothing emerged in the 1930s and glamorous cinema stars such as Marlene Dietrich and Greta Garbo began to influence what people wore. But the economic **depression** caused by the 1929 **Wall Street Crash** in the U.S.A. meant that many women could not afford the fine new fashions on offer.

Many women's outfits of the 1930s had short **boleros**. This outfit, designed by Chanel, also features a matching hat.

A longer line

The return to longer dresses that had begun at the end of the 1920s continued into the new decade. At the same time, the shapeless, boyish look disappeared and very feminine fashions became popular. High-fashion dresses were often made from bias-cut fabric—fabric that is cut diagonally across the weave and so clings to the body.

This white silk shell hat was designed by **Chanel** in 1938. It was inspired by the work of **Surrealist** artists.

These canvas platform shoes date from 1938. Women wore shoes of this type at the beach.

Suits and Schiaparelli

Another trend was the crisply tailored suit made up of a skirt ending just below the knee and a jacket with padded shoulders. Dress and jacket combinations were also popular. They were often made from tweed fabric, in the usual brown, or in more exotic colors such as pink. The most famous designer of these clothes was Elsa Schiaparelli, an Italian woman whose fashion house was based in Paris. But Chanel (see page 22) also remained fashionable.

Two swimsuits of the 1930s. Both the woman's (left) and the man's have a little "skirt" at the bottom, instead of high-cut legs.

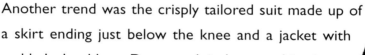

This diamond and platinum clip brooch was made in 1935. It could be worn as a single piece or split in two so that one half could be clipped to either side of a collar.

The sporting life

Men's everyday clothes of this period were much as they had been in the 1920s. But both men and women began to buy more garments specially designed for sports and for wearing on the beach. From about 1935, trend-setting men generally wore swimming trunks instead of one-piece swimming costumes.

MATERIAL MATTERS

Scientists started trying to make new fabrics in the laboratory during the late nineteenth century. They soon succeeded in making several types of artificial silk, now known as rayon (see rayon scarf below). But these were not true **synthetic** fabrics because they were made from wood-pulp, a natural substance. The first real synthetic fiber was created by American scientist Wallace Hume Carothers in 1935. He devised a chemical process that produced long, strong, silky strands. They could easily be woven to make a new fabric—**nylon**.

Fashion for All

In the 1930s, high-fashion styles became available to ordinary women. There were several reasons for this. During the Depression, Americans began to import cheap dress patterns from Paris fashion houses, instead of expensive finished garments. They used the patterns to make affordable clothes in the new styles. The film industry also played a part. In the U.S.A., "Cinema Fashions" shops were set up to sell mass-produced copies of the stars' garments. New synthetic fabrics (see left) were cheaper than natural equivalents such as silk, so garments made from them were more affordable, too.

A DRESS AND A SUIT 1930S

The woman on the left wears a typical dress of the mid-1930s. It is mid-calf length, hugs the figure closely and has a waist belt tied at the side. The shoulders are gathered on either side of the neck and the loose sleeves fall in folds to the elbow. The outfit is completed with a black pill-box hat, a half-veil, and two-tone shoes.

The woman on the right wears a Schiaparelli suit of the late 1930s. The pinched waist, padded shoulders, and severe cut are typical of the period. The velvet trim and colorful, high-necked blouse help to make the outfit more feminine. Gloves, plain **court shoes**, a high, curved hat, and a smart handbag make elegant finishing touches.

25

THE 1940S

The Second World War began in 1939, and in 1940 the Germans occupied Paris. Some fashion designers, for example Schiaparelli, left Paris for the U.S.A. Others stayed and went on working, but their designs rarely reached the outside world. As a result, Britain, the U.S.A., and many other countries developed their own fashion industries.

Materials were in short supply during the war. So in 1941, a French designer created this hat from wood shavings.

While men were away at war, women took on their jobs in factories. They wore practical clothes such as turbans and overalls.

Utility clothing

In the war, the Germans prevented cargo ships from reaching Britain, leading to shortages of all kinds. Some fabrics were in especially short supply because they were needed for military equipment. **Nylon**, for example, was used for parachutes. The government introduced clothes **rationing** in June 1941 and asked designers to create a range of cheap but stylish **utility clothing** (see far right).

American ready-to-wear

The U.S.A. entered the war in 1941, and from 1942 the use of silk, wool, and some other clothing fabrics was rationed there, too. Despite this, the country's **ready-to-wear** industry flourished. Important designers included Hattie Carnegie, who created smart suits with pleated skirts for day wear, and Norman Norell, who produced sequinned dresses and black velvet suits for evening wear. The industry remained strong after 1945, when the war ended, but Paris fought hard to win back customers.

American evening wear designer Norman Norell (see left) also created chic day dresses like this.

Men at war

In the war, civilian men generally wore wide-shouldered suits, shirts, and sturdy, lace-up shoes. British utility clothing rules limited pant widths to 19 inches and banned turn-ups. Suits of the late 1940s were much better cut (see left).

This suit dates from 1948. The wide lapels and pants with turn-ups were typical of the time.

OLD AND NEW EARLY AND LATE 1940S

The woman on the left is wearing British utility clothing. The green dress, by top designer Norman Hartnell, dates from 1943. It has a belted waist, short sleeves and wide pleats in the skirt. The dress is worn over a polka-dot red blouse with a small, rounded collar. The woman's red felt hat is perched on the rolled hairstyle typical of the era.

After the war, in 1947, French designer Christian Dior launched his Corolle Line, which became known as the New Look. Its glamour was just what many women wanted after years of strict rationing. The outfit on the right shows the look's main features— rounded shoulders, a tiny waist, and a full, flared skirt.

Le Théâtre de la Mode

The French fashion industry wanted to win back its leading role after the war. So it staged an exhibition called *Le Théâtre de la Mode* (The Fashion Theater). In 1945, 228 miniature dolls, dressed by 40 designers, were displayed at a hall in Paris. Then, in 1946, the whole collection was shown in the U.S.A. Although the clothing was greatly admired, French fashion did not really recover until the arrival of Dior's New Look (see above).

MATERIAL MATTERS

Synthetic fibers grew more popular during the 1940s, and in 1947 the plastic-coated metallic thread known as lurex was first used in clothing. Designer Elsa Schiaparelli also began to try out new forms of silk and other natural fabrics. She often had them dyed shocking pink (see left), a color that is now often associated with her.

THE 1950s

The fashions of the late 1940s continued into the 1950s. Rich women were elegant and well-groomed, wearing superbly cut clothes and shoes with **stiletto heels**. But as the decade continued, different trends developed. In particular, teenagers started to wear more informal styles in which they could dance energetically to rock-and-roll music.

Christian Dior launched the A-line in 1955. The clothes widened from top to bottom, like the sides of a letter A.

Early elegance

Christian Dior's New Look, with its small waists and wide skirts, remained fashionable for women until the mid-50s. Evening gowns of this era were particularly glamorous. They were made of costly fabrics such as silk, and decorated with beading and embroidery. Many were full-length, but the shorter "ballerina style" (see far right) was also common. Then straighter fashions were slowly introduced for day and evening wear. They included A-line dresses, skirts, and coats (see left); narrow **pencil** dresses, and Coco Chanel's classic tailored suits.

Casual styles

Among younger women especially, more casual styles developed. Many followed the film-star fashion of tight sweaters worn over pencil skirts or trousers. Another trend was the cotton dress with a wide skirt, which was ideal for doing dances such as the jive (see far right).

Teddy boys and T-shirts

Young men of the 1950s adopted various new looks. One group in Britain, Teddy boys, wore narrow drainpipe slacks, long jackets, string ties, and crêpe-soled shoes (see left). Inspired by famous film stars, others wore blue denim jeans, T-shirts, and leather jackets.

Teddy boys wore clothes in a modernized Edwardian style, copied from those made by top tailors for their rich clients.

Matching dresses and coats, worn with pearl necklaces and close-fitting hats, were popular in this era.

The bikini was invented in France in 1947 and became increasingly fashionable in the 1950s.

1956
Elvis Presley has three hits: "Heartbreak Hotel," "Hound Dog," and "Love Me Tender."

1957
European Economic Community established.

1959
Hawaii becomes the 50th state of the U.S.A.

MATERIAL MATTERS

During the 1950s, **nylon** was regularly used for stockings, but several new **synthetic** fabrics became almost as common. They included Terylene™ (known as Dacron™ in the U.S.A.), Acrilan™, and Orlon™. The new materials were lightweight and easy to wash. They did not shrink, dried quickly without creasing, and required little or no ironing. As the fabrics were so easy to care for, people were now happy to wear garments in colors that needed regular cleaning. So the new materials led to brighter clothes.

Spreading Styles

During the 1950s, many new styles by Italian designers such as Valentino spread to the rest of Europe and the U.S.A. They included men's suits with tapered pants, high-fashion knitwear, and leather shoes with very long, pointed toes. However, the most outrageous pointed shoes of that time, winkle-pickers (see above), did not spread around the world from Italy, but originated in Spanish Harlem, a poor area of New York City.

DANCING DRESSES EARLY AND LATE 1950S

The woman on the left is wearing a rose-colored evening gown of the early 1950s. It is slightly above ankle-length in the ballerina style and has a tight, strapless top over a flared, beaded, and embroidered skirt. The woman also has a flimsy, see-through stole wrapped around her shoulders. Gloves and delicate, strapped sandals complete her outfit.

The girl on the right wears a dress of the late 1950s. It is made of pink and white **gingham** cotton, and is worn over nylon petticoats stiffened with a sugar and water mixture. The dress is belted and has elasticized puff sleeves attached to the **bodice** and pulled down over the arms. The girl's ponytail hairstyle is typical of the time.

THE 1960s

Great political changes took place during the 1960s, and in 1969 men landed on the moon for the first time. Meanwhile, a new generation of young people was growing up, determined to live—and dress—in exciting new ways. They were more interested in revolutionary **ready-to-wear** clothes on sale in London boutiques than in traditional Parisian *haute couture*.

These canvas boots were designed by Barbara Hulanicki for her Biba store (see pages 32–33).

The mini-skirt revolution

The most memorable fashion of the 1960s was the mini-skirt. It was first worn in London, and probably invented by British designer Mary Quant (see page 5). Trend-setters wore the skirts with knee-length boots or ankle-strap shoes and sleek **bob** haircuts. Pantsuits also became a common fashion choice for 1960s' women.

London fashion designer Mr. Fish created this suit from American furnishing fabric in 1968.

Men in the 1960s

Many men still wore blue jeans and T-shirts, but others were more adventurous. Low-cut hipster pants in bright colors were popular. By the late 1960s, they were flared from knee to hem. Pants were often worn with shirts covered in flower or **Op Art** patterns.

Couture catches up

French *haute couture* houses were used to setting styles. But from the 1960s, they often had to follow trends developed by ready-to-wear manufacturers. Some top designers, such as Yves Saint-Laurent and André Courrèges, included mini-dresses and pantsuits in their collections. Others believed that they could not survive in this new world and closed their businesses. The rest had fewer customers than in the past, but still produced exquisitely made, highly expensive garments.

Perfectly cut suits and pill-box hats were typical of the style of Jackie Kennedy, wife of U.S. president John F. Kennedy.

"Groovy" young men of the 1960s often wore tight, flared trousers with colorful **Op Art** shirts.

MINI, MIDI, AND MAXI MID- AND LATE 1960S

The women on the left are dressed in minis of the mid-1960s. The first wears a Mary Quant design with braiding around the low waist and cuffs. The second wears a famous *haute couture* garment by Yves Saint-Laurent. Its pattern is based on a painting by Dutch artist Piet Mondrian. The third is also *haute couture* and designed by Frenchman André Courrèges. Some people claim that he, not Mary Quant, was the mini-skirt's inventor.

By the late 60s, skirts were growing longer. First the midi skirt, which ended at mid-calf, then the full-length maxi skirt, became fashionable. The garment on the right, made of painted pink chiffon, has a jagged hem that is somewhere between the two. It was created by Zandra Rhodes, a British designer of fabrics and clothes.

Space-age Style

Many 1960s' designers were interested in the race to reach the moon, and several produced collections with space themes. In his "Space Age" show of 1964, André Courrèges dressed models in hats that looked like astronauts' helmets. "Moon girl" pants made of silver and white PVC, a type of shiny plastic, were another unusual feature of the collection.

MATERIAL MATTERS

Designers experimented with all sorts of new materials in the 1960s. No one was more daring than Spanish designer Paco Rabanne. He made garments from patches of plastic, stones, and ostrich feathers, as well as metal plates and chains. The amazing metal clothes (see left) often looked like suits of armor.

1973
U.S. troops withdraw from Vietnam.
Yom Kippur War between Israel, and an alliance of Egypt and Syria.

1973–1974
Price rise in oil from Arab countries leads to energy crisis in U.S.A. and Europe.

1975
Vietnam War ends.

THE 1970S

A great mixture of fashion trends emerged in the 1970s. Some British designers based their collections on fashions of the 1930s. American designers created sleek new styles, while the Japanese introduced startlingly different clothing shapes. Meanwhile, groups such as **hippies** and **punks** ignored high fashion to create unusual outfits of their own.

Designer styles

One of the most inventive designers in 1970s' Britain was Barbara Hulanicki (see far right). In the U.S.A., Ralph Lauren, famous for his Polo menswear, produced his first women's garments in 1971. Lauren's fashions were usually elegant and simple, but his 1978 collection was based on clothes of the American West. In France, Karl Lagerfeld made smart outfits from natural fabrics such as wool.

Enter the Japanese

Many designers from Japan made their mark in the West during the 1970s. Among the most important was Issey Miyake, who held his first fashion show in New York in 1971. He combined a knowledge of Japanese clothing with tailoring skills learned in Paris. The loose garments he created were often layered and draped in unusual ways.

Hippie chic

The hippie movement reached its height in the early 1970s. Its members took pride in their individuality so they created unique costumes made up of "ethnic" garments from all over the world. Favorite items included Afghan coats (embroidered sheepskin coats), South American ponchos, and caftans. Flared slacks and colorful T-shirts were also popular.

From 1971, there was a brief craze for hotpants—short, tight shorts with a bib attached.

Platform shoes, which had been popular many years earlier (see pages 24–25), made a comeback during the 1970s.

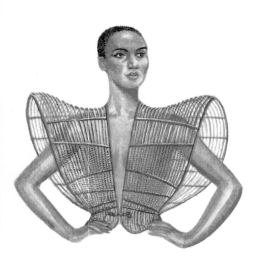

This bodice was created by Issey Miyake (see right). He used all sorts of new materials, from rigid plastics to textured wools.

Ralph Lauren's most famous styles were based on the casual clothing worn by wealthy British and Americans in the 1920s.

Hippies mixed many styles and colors. Both men and women wore long strings of beads and painted flowers on their faces.

1976
Anglo-French supersonic airliner Concorde makes its first commercial flight.

1978
Camp David talks in the U.S.A. lead to agreement between Egypt and Israel.

1979
The first personal computers go on sale.

MATERIAL MATTERS

Hippies loved to wear T-shirts and other clothes made of tie-dye fabrics. They were produced by tying string tightly round plain cloth in various places, then soaking it in dye. The dye did not color the string-covered areas, so patterns of white rings were left in the cloth (see right).

Fitness Fashions

During the late 1970s, fitness became fashionable. People began to work out at gyms and jog round parks, as well as continuing to dance the night away at discotheques. Designers quickly spotted the trend and began to produce jogging suits, **leotards**, and other special clothes for exercise wear. Among the most famous was American Norma Kamali, who used fabrics such as parachute **nylon** for her fitness garments.

ROMANCE AND REBELLION
1970S

At her Biba store in London, Barbara Hulanicki sold flowing, romantic garments inspired by **Art Nouveau** (see page 21), **Art Deco**, and the glamorous styles of 1930s' Hollywood. Popular colors were black, brown, and plum. The woman on the left is wearing a typical Biba outfit—a full-length dress made of satin trimmed with gold sequins, and a matching short jacket. She carries a gold clutch bag.

The rebellious punks of the mid-1970s dressed to shock. The punk man on the far right wears black jeans, a leather jacket, and a leopard print T-shirt that almost matches his hair. The punk woman wears leather pants and a Union Jack vest. Her dyed blonde hair is arranged in stiff rays around her head.

33

LATE TWENTIETH CENTURY

During the 1980s, rich professionals began power dressing (see below). Young people wore a fast-changing variety of street styles. Clothes were generally much softer in the 1990s, but on the street and the catwalk, the range of fashionable shapes and colors steadily increased.

Power dressing

In the early 1980s, businesses and banks were doing well. Men wanted to appear powerful and dynamic at work, so designers such as Italian Giorgio Armani and American Calvin Klein made suits that created the right look. Jackets were **double-breasted** with heavily padded shoulders. Dress pants were expertly cut and creased. Women also adopted this power-dressing style (see left).

Street style

Young people of the 1980s developed many new fashion styles, often inspired by the bands that they watched. For example, jogging suits and athletic shoes became popular items of clothing after they were worn on stage by black artists. New youth magazines, now for men as well as women, included photographs of inventive outfits worn by people on the street and in clubs. These styles then spread, and were even copied by some *haute couture* designers.

Into the 1990s

In the 1990s, matching dresses and jackets in more feminine styles became popular with businesswomen, while men's suits returned to a more natural shape. Many top designers, such as Ralph Lauren, aimed to produce classic, easy-to-wear clothes (see page 32). But others dazzled the world with wild creations based on everything from nineteenth-century **crinolines** to kilts.

Female power-dressers usually wore skirt or pantsuits. The jackets had padded shoulders.

Frenchman Jean-Paul Gaultier's daring designs are influenced by street styles. They include this 1983 corset dress.

Rap singers helped to make athletic shoes and jogging suits fashionable far from the sports field.

Shoe designer Patrick Cox created the highly successful Wannabe range of loafers in 1993. One style is shown above.

Designer Labels

The *haute couture* industry (see page 11) has survived, but few can afford the garments it produces. For this reason, many top designers also create less costly **ready-to-wear** ranges and even more affordable diffusion ranges. Diffusion ranges include everything from sneakers to perfumes, and have filled the streets with designer labels. But customers no longer depend on top designers for the latest styles. Retail stores produce cheaper versions of catwalk fashions within weeks.

MATERIAL MATTERS

Chiffon—a delicate see-through fabric often made of silk—was one of the high-fashion materials of the year 2000. Designers used it for blouses, skirts, and wraps, in colors such as pale pink and blue. Another favorite was Lycra™, which had been popular since the 1970s. Then it was used mainly for sportswear because it stretches easily, so lets people move freely. But by the end of the twentieth century, it was included in more everyday garments such as blouses, skirts, and trousers.

RUNWAY CREATIONS 1990S–2000

Retro styles based on earlier periods of history were common in the 1990s. The first outfit on the left dates from 1994 and was designed by Englishman Paul Smith. It is based on the Teddy boy outfits of the 1950s (see page 28). The second outfit, from 1999, is by Frenchman Hubert de Givenchy. It combines a nineteenth-century-style crinoline with modern leather pants.

Trends for the new millennium include bright colors and prints. The pink dress on the right appeared in the first fashion shows of 2000. It was created by the design house Jean Muir, whose founder produced clothes in simple, classic styles.

AMERICAN AND EUROPEAN TRADITIONAL COSTUME

A father and son from the Quechua people of Peru. Both wear ponchos over European-style pants.

While fashions change almost daily in the West, people in many other parts of the world still wear age-old traditional costumes. Inhabitants of some countries wear fashionable garments in their daily lives and folk costumes on special occasions. On this spread you can find out about traditional clothing in the Americas and Europe.

South and Central America

In South and Central America, many people wear a mixture of garments. They dress in some styles once worn by the original Indian inhabitants and others worn by the Spanish and Portuguese people who conquered the region from the sixteenth century. In Peru, for example, men often wear a cape-like garment, called a poncho, over European-style pants. In Mexico, women put old-style shoulder capes over blouses, which were introduced by the Spanish.

North America

American Indians, the original inhabitants of North America, wore a wide variety of garments. These varied from cotton loincloths in Florida to animal skin shirts on the Great Plains. When European settlers spread across the continent, they made American Indians wear European-style clothing. But the ancient costumes did not die out and people have begun to wear them again.

Modern American Indians celebrate their cultures at events called powwows. There they wear costumes based on traditional styles.

Europe

In the past, ordinary Europeans wore folk costumes for festivals and weddings. Styles were very varied, but were often ornate and decorated with colorful embroidery (see far right). Many of these costumes are becoming rare, but some people are working hard to stop them from dying out.

Many rainforest peoples of Brazil still dress in traditional clothing. This Karaja Indian wears a spectacular headdress shaped like a giant halo.

SCOTLAND, SPAIN, AND SCANDINAVIA

Many Scottish people still wear traditional costume for occasions such as highland games. The main men's garment is the kilt (see left). As shown here, it is worn with a pouch known as a sporran on top. The color and pattern of the tartan from which a kilt is made depends on the clan to which the man belongs.

Women of Spain's Andalusia region, in the South, wear ruffled dresses like the one on the left for festivals. The dresses sway as the women perform flamenco dances. Their male partners wear tight pants and short jackets.

The people of Scandinavian countries have kept their folk traditions alive and special dance groups wear traditional costumes. The Danish woman on the right wears a beautifully embroidered skirt and **bodice**.

AFRICAN AND ASIAN TRADITIONAL COSTUME

On these two pages, you can read about some of the traditional costumes worn in parts of Africa, the Middle East, and Asia.

North and West African costumes

Arabs brought the religion of Islam to North Africa in the twelfth century and many men there now wear turbans and Arab-style tunics called *djellabahs*. Women are expected to dress modestly, so generally cover themselves in full-length, long-sleeved robes and veils when they go out. In West African countries such as Cameroon, women's costume is often a brightly printed blouse, long wrap-around skirt, and headcloth. Men wear long robes, or pants and sleeveless tunics.

Southern and East African costumes

In some areas of Southern Africa, such as in parts of Namibia, men and women wear only loincloths or short skirts. In much of South Africa itself, Western clothing has replaced traditional tribal styles, but they have not died out totally. Zulu men dress in skin and feather war costumes for special occasions. The Masai women of East Africa wear deep, beaded collars and brightly colored cloaks. In the Muslim areas of the Sudan, long, Arab-style robes are common.

Middle Eastern costumes

In much of the Middle East, Muslim Arab men dress in long, loose tunics and either turbans or headcloths called *keffiyeh*. Women wear tunics, too, over which they drape long, full cloaks when they go out. It is also common for them to veil their heads and faces. Although garments are similar throughout the Middle East, each country has its own special designs.

Many women from the Ivory Coast in West Africa wear tops and wrap-around skirts made from boldly printed fabric.

Masai women from parts of East Africa wear bright fabric wraps or tunics and beaded collars.

This man from Cameroon, West Africa, wears a headcloth and a long robe called a *gandoura* over baggy pants.

This Saudi Arabian man wears a plain white *thob* tunic with a *gumbaz* coat on the top. His *keffiyeh* headcloth is held in place with head ropes.

ASIAN STYLES

In parts of Indonesia, both men and women dress in wrap-around skirts called sarongs. As shown here (top left), women wear blouses called *kebayas* on the top. They are held in place with wide waist sashes. Indonesian clothing is often made from batik fabrics (see below).

In many regions of India, women dress in long saris wound over short-sleeved **bodices** called *cholis*. But in other areas, for example the north-western region of the Punjab, loose *salwar* pants and a long, shirt-like top called a *kameez* (see left) are more commonly worn.

When China became Communist in 1949, many people began to wear Mao suits (see right). Their plainness emphasized the equality of all people and the need to take life seriously. Now Western clothes are becoming more common. But far from the capital, Beijing, non-Chinese minorities still wear a huge variety of traditional costumes.

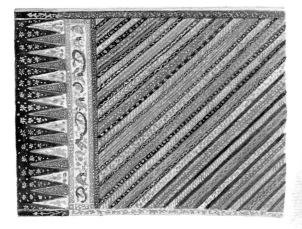

MATERIAL MATTERS

Batik fabrics are produced by putting wax onto cloth in various places, then soaking it in dye. The areas covered by the wax resist the dye and so remain their original color. As a result, a pattern is created. Dyers on the Indonesian island of Java use a special tool called a *canting* to make their batiks. It has a spout through which they pour the wax to make detailed patterns. In this way, they produce lovely fabrics like this example (see left).

MATERIAL MATTERS

Over the past 200 years, people have devised many new ways of weaving and printing material. At the same time, they have invented many new textiles. Now designers, manufacturers, and clothes buyers can choose from a range of natural and **synthetic** fabrics.

At first, no one outside France knew how to make Jacquard looms like these. Then, in 1820, a spy was sent from England to find out. By the mid-nineteenth century, the looms were in use all over Britain.

Jacquard looms

One major cloth-making development occurred at the very start of the Modern period. In 1801, Frenchman Joseph Marie Jacquard introduced a system of punched cards designed to help produce patterned fabrics. A special Jacquard attachment was fixed on top of the loom to hold these cards. The cards automatically guided the threads into the correct positions to make the pattern. Previously a weaver's assistant called a drawboy had to do this work by hand.

Automated looms

During the nineteenth century, **power looms** driven by steam or water gradually replaced hand looms. Then, in the twentieth century, electrically powered looms were introduced. Now looms are controlled by computers, which scan the patterns required, then electronically deliver instructions to the machines. This technology is mainly used in rich, industrialized countries. Elsewhere in the world, fabric is still woven on hand looms.

Some Navajo Indians of the Southwestern U.S.A. still weave woolen fabrics on upright hand looms. This example dates from the nineteenth century.

In this scene from the mid-1800s, a man is operating a roller-printing machine. The designs on the cloth are clearly visible.

Printing techniques

Modern methods of printing patterns onto plain fabric include roller printing, developed by Scotsman Thomas Bell in 1783. It involves passing the fabric over one or more rollers etched with a design and covered in dye. Several varieties of this technique are still used today. Screen printing (see left) began in the 1920s. At first it was done only by hand, but automated screen printing is now widely used in factories.

New fabrics

The first major new fabric of modern times was rayon (see page 25). It was invented by Englishman Joseph Swan in 1883, but first made commercially by Frenchman Hilaire de Chardonnet. Viscose, a kind of rayon, arrived in the early twentieth century. The creation of **nylon** in 1935 led to the development of more synthetic fabrics, including polyesters such as Terylene™ and acrylics such as Orlon™ (see page 29).

Expanding elastic

The development of elastic fabrics began in 1820, when Englishman Thomas Hancock produced a cloth containing rubber. At first, elastic was mainly used for panels in shoes and boots. But in the 1920s, manufacturers began to put it in women's undergarments, making them far more flexible than the old whalebone corsets. Some modern fabrics, such as Lycra™, contain artificial, non-rubber elastic.

Old and new

In recent years, scientists have developed many new textiles with special properties, for example "breathable" fabrics that allow perspiration to escape. Soon, there will even be fabrics that contain electronic devices (see right). But many people still prefer natural materials that have stood the test of time—wool, cotton, **linen**, and, of course, sumptuous silk.

Screen printing involves first placing the material to be printed in a shallow tray (screen). A piece of fine-meshed gauze, coated in some areas with a special varnish, is then placed over the top. When dye is applied to the gauze, it cannot get through the varnish, so only some areas of the fabric below are colored. In this way a pattern is created.

Rayon manufacturers held an Artificial Silk Exhibition in 1926 to advertise their new material. Visitors were allowed to touch the garments on the models.

This corset with built-in bra dates from the mid-twentieth century. The long, elasticized panels were designed to mold the body into shape.

The very latest garments have built-in electronics. Sewn inside this jacket is a remote control that operates a mobile phone and an MP3 player.

MODERN ACCESSORIES

People of the Modern era wore all sorts of accessories. Some were practical items, others purely decorative. As the Modern era continues into the twenty-first century, accessories are as popular as ever. You have already learned about some Modern accessories earlier in this book. This chart tells you more, and makes it easy to compare the jewelry, footwear, and headwear worn at many times and in many places.

	JEWELRY	FOOTWEAR	HEADWEAR
EARLY 19TH-CENTURY FRANCE	Rich women wear jewelry inspired by the styles of Ancient Greece and Rome. A set of matching jewelry is called a parure. A typical example includes a tiara, necklace, earrings, bracelets, and a jeweled clasp.	Many Frenchwomen wear slipper-style shoes loosely based on Greek and Roman styles. Flat, laced ankle boots also become popular. During the Napoleonic Wars, many men wear military-style boots.	Men wear cocked tricorne or bicorne hats. Top hats made of beaver felt are also popular. Women wear feather-trimmed bonnets tied under the chin with ribbons.
LATE 19TH-CENTURY FRANCE	During the reign of Napoleon III, women's jewelry is even more grand. To go about in high society, women need several parures, one made of diamonds and others of colored stones such as sapphires.	Elastic is first made in the mid-nineteenth century (see page 41), and men start to wear short boots with elastic side panels. Women wear laced or side-buttoned boots or heeled mules.	Among men, the top hat, made of black silk instead of felt, is still fashionable. From the 1880s, women start to wear a variety of elaborately decorated hats instead of bonnets. Many have light face veils.
EARLY 19TH-CENTURY BRITAIN	British women mainly follow French jewelry fashions. They often wear full parures at night, and earrings with a matching brooch or pendant in the daytime.	British women wear plain, flat slippers like those popular in France. Later in the century, shoes become more fussy with all sorts of trimmings. High military boots are fashionable for men.	Bonnets are the most usual form of women's headwear. One style is the poke bonnet, with a brim extending forward over the face. Turbans are also popular. For men, the top hat replaces cocked hats.
LATE 19TH-CENTURY BRITAIN	Much British jewelry is mass-produced, using paste stones and cheap metal. Women wear chatelaines and lockets. Men wear fob watches and decorative **cravat** pins.	Women continue to wear flat, laced boots and slipper-style shoes. But then, as in France, heels make a comeback. Oxford shoes and elastic-sided ankle boots are popular new styles for men.	Some women wear flat, straw "shepherdess" hats, but elaborate hats piled high with feathers, flowers, and lace become more common. Men wear top hats, and bowler hats for more informal occasions.
19TH-CENTURY USA	Many rich American women wear European jewelry that they buy in London and Paris. Some also spend their money in the famous Tiffany and Co. jewelry shop in New York City.	Except in the West, most American shoes and boots are European in style. Some are shipped to the U.S.A. from abroad. Others are made there by skilled craftsmen, especially after the Civil War.	American hats also follow European fashions. Many rich women bring hats back from the 1867 Paris International Exhibition. Hats are often stored in bandboxes printed with colorful patterns.

JEWELRY	FOOTWEAR	HEADWEAR	
Art Nouveau styles of jewelry are popular. The exotic colors and shapes of Ballets Russes designs (see page 21) also influence jewelry styles. Popular items include deep chokers.	Women begin to wear heeled fabric or leather **court shoes** decorated with buckles. Men still wear short boots with elastic panels or side buttons. In the U.S.A., boots with pointed toes are popular.	Women's hats are tall, with many trimmings. They are held in place by decorative hat pins. The Homburg hat and the trilby are popular for men. Top hats are worn for formal occasions.	**EARLY 20TH-CENTURY EUROPE**
Art Deco jewelry is popular. So are Egyptian-style pieces after the discovery of Pharaoh Tutankhamun's tomb in 1922. Long ropes of pearls with tassels at the end are draped over the new, straight dresses.	1920s' short skirts put women's footwear on display as never before. Most women's shoes are slender with high heels and single straps or T-bars. Men wear black or brown lace-ups.	The tight-fitting, brimless **cloche** is popular for women. It is worn pulled down over a short hairstyle such as the **shingle**. Among men, top hats become rare and felt hats are more popular.	**1920s**
Geometric Art Deco designs are popular for much of the 1930s. Clip brooches that can be divided in two and screw-on earrings for unpierced ears are important new jewelry items.	Women still wear strapped shoes, but high-fronted, laced shoes are now the height of fashion. Both men and women begin to wear sandals in summer. Women's sandals often have platform soles.	Women wear a variety of hats, usually pulled down to one side on the head. Some are almost like skullcaps, while others are shaped like large plates. Men wear top hats, felt hats, or bowlers.	**1930s**
Platinum, once a popular jewelry metal, is not used during World War II since it is needed for machinery. Gold becomes more common. After the war, diamond brooches and chains of gold links are fashionable.	To prevent the waste of leather, wartime governments limit heel heights. After the war, women's shoes become glamorous again, with high heels and ankle straps. Men wear flat lace-up styles.	Women's hats of the early 1940s are often made of molded felt. Many men still wear felt hats, but increasing numbers choose not to cover their heads at all.	**1940s**
Stunning, multi-rowed necklaces of diamonds and other precious stones adorn the glamorous ballgowns of the 1950s. Short strings of pearls and round pearl clip earrings are also popular.	**Stiletto**-heeled shoes are the most fashionable shoes for women. Many men still wear flat lace-ups, but among the young, winkle-pickers are the height of cool.	Many women's hats are made of artificial flowers and fruits. Face veils are often attached. Women who want to look like film stars drape silk scarves over their heads and wear sunglasses.	**1950s**
Plastic is a popular—and cheap—jewelry material. Now ordinary women can afford bracelets, necklaces, and earrings in many colors. Rich women still wear jewelry made of precious stones and metals.	High-heeled, knee-length boots and T-bar shoes are fashionable footwear styles for women. Men favor Chelsea boots—leather ankle boots with elastic side panels and small heels.	Hats are not popular, at least not among the trend-setting young. Sometimes fashionable men and women perch berets on their heads. In the U.S.A., Jackie Kennedy (see page 30) popularizes the pill-box hat.	**1960s**
Hippies, both men and women, drape long strands of beads over their clothes. **Punks** prefer more outrageous jewelry, such as safety pins and chains. Older women continue to wear more traditional styles.	Platform shoes make a comeback among both women and men. **Hippies** generally prefer flat leather sandals, while punks often wear lace-up boots with thick soles. Athletic shoes become popular, too.	Hats are not popular, but there are many new hairstyles. Some African-Americans cut their hair into "Afros," that is bushy halos around their heads. Punks form their hair into spikes.	**1970s**
Large items of jewelry are worn by some businesswomen to emphasize their wealth. Now, many different styles, from delicate beaded necklaces to heavy gold chains, are all popular at the same time.	Athletic shoes are the most common type of casual footwear. Among other styles, Patrick Cox's Wannabe loafers are popular, but ultra-feminine shoes with stiletto or kitten heels are high-fashion, too.	Few people regularly wear hats. Some women wear elaborate styles to weddings, where men occasionally appear in top hats. In winter, pull-on wool hats are popular, and in summer straw hats for shade.	**LATE 20TH CENTURY**

MAPS OF THE MODERN WORLD

The main pages of this book refer to many different places all around the world. They include cities, regions, countries, and continents as well as natural features. The maps on these pages show where many of these places are or were.

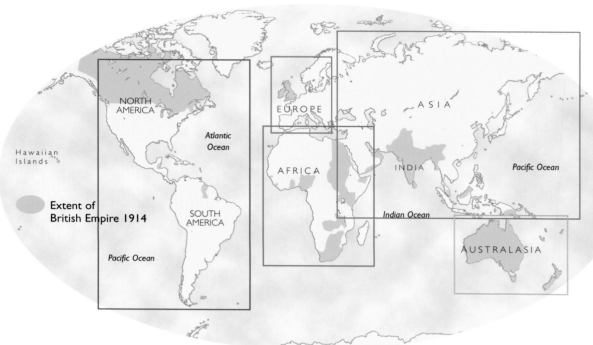

NORTH AMERICA

EUROPE

ASIA

Atlantic Ocean

AFRICA

INDIA

Pacific Ocean

Hawaiian Islands

Indian Ocean

Extent of British Empire 1914

SOUTH AMERICA

AUSTRALASIA

Pacific Ocean

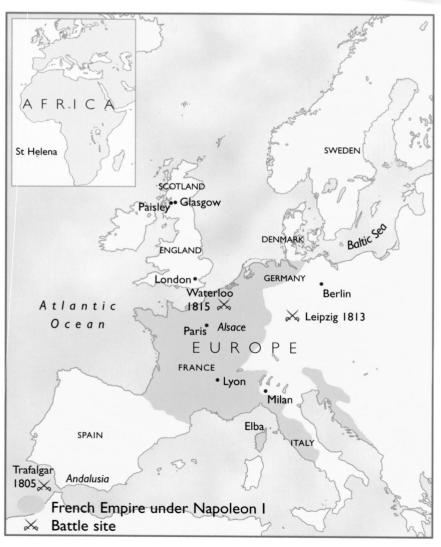

AFRICA

St Helena

SCOTLAND

Paisley • • Glasgow

SWEDEN

ENGLAND

DENMARK

Baltic Sea

London •

GERMANY

Berlin •

Atlantic Ocean

Waterloo 1815 ⚔

⚔ Leipzig 1813

Paris • • Alsace

EUROPE

FRANCE

• Lyon

• Milan

Elba

SPAIN

ITALY

Trafalgar 1805 ⚔

Andalusia

French Empire under Napoleon I

⚔ **Battle site**

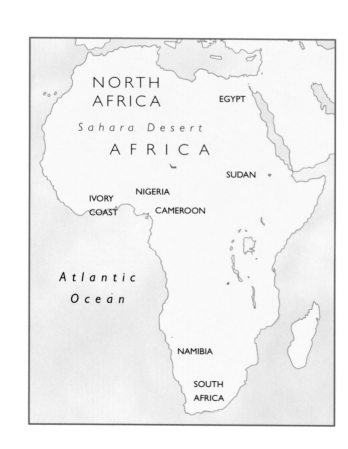

NORTH AFRICA

EGYPT

Sahara Desert

AFRICA

SUDAN

NIGERIA

IVORY COAST

CAMEROON

Atlantic Ocean

NAMIBIA

SOUTH AFRICA

The world map (left) highlights areas that each of the more detailed maps covers. The general key below and the special keys on the maps provide more information. Great empires that existed at certain times in history, as well as major historical events such as the American Civil War, are also mentioned in the previous pages. The maps here show the boundaries of empires and the places where major events took place.

Key:
- U.S.A. following independence 1783
- Louisiana Purchase 1803
- Gadsden Purchase 1853
- Division of Confederate states (South) and Union states (North)

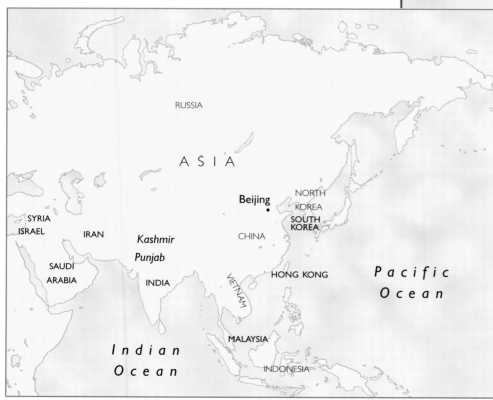

General key to place names

A F R I C A	Continent name
FRANCE	Country name
Punjab	Region name
Glasgow	City name
Sahara Desert	Natural feature

45

GLOSSARY

Art Deco A style of art and architecture that was originally popular during the late 1920s and 1930s. Art Deco designs often include geometric shapes in bright colors.

Art Nouveau A style of art and architecture that was originally popular from about 1890 to 1910. It often featured swirling shapes and images of natural objects such as plants, leaves, and flowers.

bandanna A large handkerchief made of cotton, linen, or silk. Cowboys tied bandannas around their necks.

bob A neat hairstyle for women in which the hair is cut quite short to frame the face, then turned under all the way around.

bodice A tight-fitting garment worn on the upper part of a woman's body.

bolero A type of women's jacket that finishes above the waist.

buckskin A type of dark yellow suede made from deerskin.

bustle A device made of horsehair, wire, or other material that women in the late nineteenth century wore under their skirts to make them stick out at the back.

cage crinoline A metal framework that women in the mid-nineteenth century wore under their skirts to make them sweep outwards from a very narrow waist to a very wide hem.

calico Plain, unbleached cotton.

chemise A knee-length, sleeveless tunic that was worn by women as an undergarment.

Chesterfield A style of men's overcoat that became popular in the 1840s. Chesterfields had velvet collars and buttons that were hidden by a strip of fabric. They were named after the Earl of Chesterfield.

cloche A style of women's hat that was popular during the 1920s. The hat was bell-shaped (*cloche* is French for "bell") and fitted tightly on the head.

colony A country that is occupied and ruled by people from another country.

court shoe A style of women's shoe that is cut low at the front and has no fastenings across the arch of the foot. Court shoes usually have small- or medium-sized heels.

cravat A long strip of linen that nineteenth-century men tied around their shirts at the neck.

crinoline A type of cotton or linen petticoat padded with horsehair and stiffened with whalebone. Crinolines were worn under skirts from the 1840s to produce a sweeping curve from waist to hem. They were replaced by cage crinolines in the mid-1850s.

cutaway tailcoat A type of tailcoat worn in the nineteenth century that is cut straight across the front at waist level, then falls to two, knee-length tails at the back.

depression A period of low business growth and high unemployment.

double-breasted A term used to describe a jacket with sides that overlap at the front so that there are two layers of fabric on top of one another. Double-breasted jackets are fastened with two rows of buttons.

drawers An undergarment with pant legs but made of light material such as cotton. Drawers often finish just below the knee.

Early Modern era The era of history that followed the Middle Ages. It started in about 1492, when explorer Christopher Columbus first reached the Americas, and finished at the end of the eighteenth century, at about the time of the French Revolution.

Empire line A term that describes garments worn in France, Britain, and other parts of Europe during the period of the first French Empire (1804–1814). For women, these were highwaisted dresses, and for men tail coats, waistcoats, and tight britches.

fichu A type of scarf draped around the neck of a dress. *Fichus* were often made of white muslin.

flax A type of blue-flowered plant whose stems are used to make linen.

French Revolution The period of French history from 1789 to 1799, during which the monarchy was overthrown and a new form of government set up.

frock coat A type of men's coat worn in the nineteenth century that has a "skirt" sewn on at the waist. The skirt is the same length all the way round and usually has a vent (split) at the back.

gingham Checked, or sometimes striped, cotton fabric.

haute couture The best and most expensive type of fashion, created by top designers and tailored to fit individual customers. The term also refers to the high-fashion business.

hippie   A person who, especially during the 1960s and 1970s, rejected the usual customs and values of society. Both male and female hippies grew their hair long and wore clothes from all over the world.

Industrial Revolution   The period from about the mid-eighteenth to the mid-nineteenth century when Western Europe and the U.S.A. changed from being places where most people worked on the land to places where most people worked in factories.

kimono   A traditional Japanese garment worn by men and women. It is usually long and loose with full-length sleeves, and is fastened around the waist with an obi sash.

knickerbockers   A type of baggy britches (short pants) that finish in a band at the knee.

leg-of-mutton sleeve   A style of sleeve that tapers from a wide shoulder to a narrow wrist. It is so called because it looks like the leg of a sheep (mutton is sheep meat).

leotard   A close-fitting garment shaped like a swimsuit, but with long sleeves and a back.

linen   A fabric made from the stem fibers of the flax plant.

linsey-woolsey   A rough, hard-wearing fabric that is a mixture of linen and wool or cotton.

lounge suit   A man's suit of thigh-length, straight-hemmed jacket, and matching pants. Lounge suits were first worn in the 1870s and are still popular, although the cut has changed.

moccasin   A flat, pull-on style of shoe made of soft leather that completely covers the front of the foot.

morning coat   A type of man's coat with a single row of buttons, tapered sides, and rounded tails.

morning dress   The garments that together make up formal daywear for men—a morning coat, dark slacks, and a top hat.

muslin   A type of plain, fine cotton fabric.

nylon   A synthetic material whose silky fibers can be made into fabric.

obi   A sash worn around a kimono.

Op Art   A style of modern art that uses bold, abstract patterns.

pencil   In fashion, a term used to describe a dress or skirt that is narrow, like the shape of a pencil, and so tight-fitting.

polonaise   A style of woman's dress with a tight bodice and an overskirt pulled up to reveal an underskirt.

power loom   A loom powered by steam or water rather than human hands and feet.

punk   A person who, especially during the late 1970s, acted and dressed in a way designed to shock. Many punks were young, wore pants and jackets adorned with chains, and styled their hair in outrageous ways.

rationing   The practice of allowing people only limited supplies of clothes, food, and other goods. Rationing is often introduced by governments during wartime.

ready-to-wear   A term used to describe garments made to standard sizes and bought from shops, not tailored to fit individual customers like *haute couture*.

Renaissance   The period of history during which European men and women rediscovered the learning of the ancient world while making great new advances in art and science. It lasted from about 1350 to 1550. *Renaissance* is French for "rebirth."

shingle   A short hairstyle worn by some 1920s' women. It was similar to the Eton crop, but less severe.

stiletto heels   Very high heels on women's shoes. They are quite wide at the top, but narrow almost to a point at the bottom.

stock   A type of stiffened neckcloth worn by nineteenth-century men that was fastened with a tie or buckle at the back.

Surrealist   A word that describes a style of art popular in the 1920s and 1930s. Surrealist art put all sorts of unrelated objects next to one another, for example, a lobster and a telephone, and often tried to create images like those seen in dreams.

synthetic   A term used to describe a dye or fabric made artificially by combining chemicals in a laboratory, rather than occurring naturally.

tailcoat   Any of various styles of man's coat that have two tails—long, pointed sections of cloth divided by a split from waist to hem—at the back.

utility clothing   Simple clothing that uses a minimum of fabric, fastenings and trimmings. It is usually designed and worn during wars when many goods are in short supply.

Wall Street Crash   A financial crisis triggered by panic selling on the stock exchange in Wall Street, New York, in late October 1929.

INDEX

THE
DEVILS
WHO LEARNED TO BE
GOOD

THE
DEVILS
WHO LEARNED TO BE
GOOD

MICHAEL McCURDY

JOY STREET BOOKS

LITTLE, BROWN AND COMPANY   BOSTON   TORONTO

Library of Congress Cataloging-in-Publication Data
McCurdy, Michael.
    The devils who learned to be good.

    Summary: After feeding two starving beggars, an old
Russian soldier receives a magical flour sack and deck
of playing cards which help him to remove some pesky
devils from the Tsar's palace.
    [1. Folklore — Soviet Union]   I. Title.
PZ8.1.M157De 1987   398.2'1'0947   87-4203
ISBN 0-316-55527-4

DESIGNED BY JEANNE ABBOUD

Published simultaneously in Canada
by Little, Brown & Company (Canada) Limited
PRINTED IN THE UNITED STATES

TO

Heather and Mark

An old Russian soldier, having served in the Tsar's army for thirty-five years, had nothing to show for it but two dry loaves of bread and the clothes upon his back. He hugged his companions good-bye, thinking of the celebration there would be in his village upon his return, and set off toward home. He was quite merry, and he sang aloud as he walked briskly through the Russian countryside. It was good to be going home.

Presently he came upon a beggar, dressed in miserable

rags. The beggar was clearly hungry, and the old soldier, possessing a generous nature, gave him one of the loaves of bread. To thank the soldier, the beggar pulled from his tattered pocket a worn deck of playing cards.

"With these cards," he said, "you will always win. Take them, and go with God's mercy!"

The soldier took the cards, put them in his own pocket, said good-bye to the beggar, and continued on his way.

It wasn't long before he spotted another beggar sitting by the roadside. This poor fellow was in even worse condition

than the last, and he too begged for food. Now, the soldier was troubled, for he knew that if he gave this beggar his last loaf of bread, then he himself might go hungry. But what if the two beggars met up with each other, and the first told the second that he had received bread? Surely, it would only make the second beggar feel worse than he already did. So, trusting in God's mercy, the soldier offered the poor man his other loaf. Overjoyed, the beggar gave the soldier his blessing, then handed him what appeared to be an old flour sack.

"Take this sack," said the beggar, "and if you see anything you wish to catch, just open the sack, tell whatever it is to climb inside, and do with the creature what you will."

"Thank you," said the soldier, and he tucked the sack among his belongings and continued on his way. It wasn't long before he felt hungry and tired from the long walk over rough terrain. He sat down beside the edge of a little pond, where he noticed three fat ducks in the water. He suddenly remembered the old sack and what the second beggar had told him. Opening the sack, he shouted at the top of his voice: "You beautiful ducks, come at once into my sack!"

In an instant the three ducks flew up out of the water and into the sack, whereupon the soldier tied the sack, put it on his shoulder, and continued on his journey.

Presently he came to a town. He looked for the finest inn he could find and called out to the innkeeper, "Here are three fat ducks. I'll have one of them tonight for my dinner. I'll give you the second for your finest wine. And the third I shall give you for preparing my meal."

The innkeeper readily agreed, and soon the soldier was sitting at a big oaken table, eating a delicious roast duck, and drinking the best wine the town could offer. When the soldier had finished, he leaned back contentedly, lit his little clay pipe, and looked out the window. Across the street was the grandest palace he had ever seen. The carving of the stonework and the great wooden door were a marvel to behold. But what really surprised him was that in all the many windows there was not one pane of glass that was not broken.

"Tell me," said the soldier, "why does that fine palace have so many broken windows?"

"It's a fine palace, to be sure," answered the innkeeper. "The Tsar himself built it, but no one has ever been able to live in it. Devils have taken it over. They shout and yell and play their fiddles. Why, the town itself is not fit for anyone who wants a decent night's sleep!"

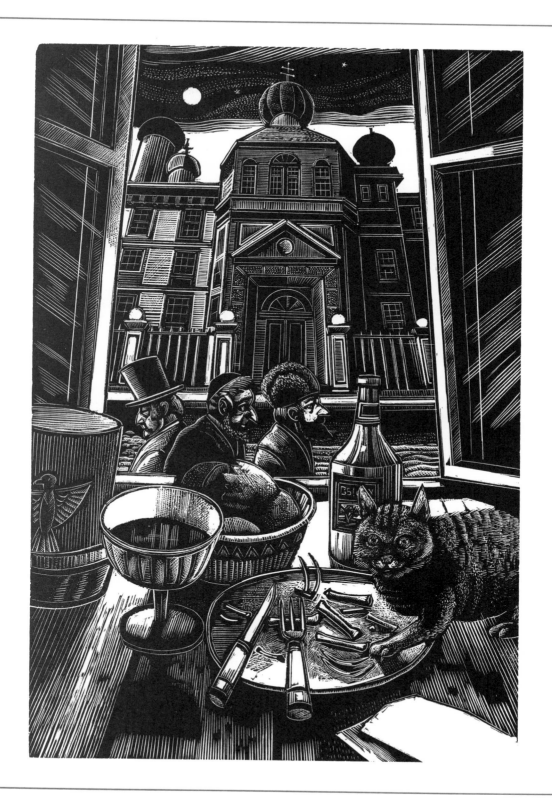

The soldier said farewell to the innkeeper and went in search of the Tsar, who happened to be spending the week at his hunting lodge nearby. Bold as brass, the old soldier entered the lodge, walked past the guards, saluted the Tsar, and offered his services.

"Your Majesty," said the soldier, "will you let me spend the night in your palace, so that I may drive out the devils who have taken it over?"

"You are not the first to ask," said the Tsar. "More than one fool has dared to spend the night there, but everyone who did has wished he had not asked."

"I have served God and Your Majesty for thirty-five years," said the soldier. "I truly believe that I can outwit those devils."

The Tsar finally gave in. Before he could change his mind, the soldier gathered up his belongings and entered the large, dark building. There was no one to be seen. Finding a comfortable spot on the floor in the biggest room, he sat down, lit up his pipe and a small candle, and waited patiently for something to happen.

At exactly midnight, he heard the most dreadful noises coming from the stairway and outer hall. All of a sudden, the big door burst open and the room filled up with noisy, grotesque devils. They were shouting. They were playing fiddles. They were dancing. In fact, they acted as if they owned the place! For a moment, they didn't see the soldier, sitting as he was in a corner of the room. When they did,

they stopped short and stared at him rudely, for they had
no manners.

"What are you doing there, old soldier?" asked the devils. "Put your pipe down and play a game of cards with
us!"

"I would indeed enjoy a game of cards," said the soldier,
"if you will play with *my* cards."

"Deal the cards!" screamed all the devils with excitement, for it's a well-known fact that no devil can resist a good card game. They put out their money for the winner to take, while the soldier put out some coins the Tsar had kindly given him.

The soldier won the first game easily — and the second as well. Before long he had won all the money the devils had with them. After pouring it into the deep pockets of his greatcoat, he sat back contentedly and lit his pipe once more.

The devils were mystified. They were very clever and had never lost at cards before.

"Look here, soldier," said the eldest, "we happen to have two baskets of silver and three baskets of gold. Put out the money you won, and we'll put out our silver and gold. The winner of the next ten games will take all."

"Let's see the gold and silver," said the soldier. Two of the youngest devils were sent for it. They staggered back under the weight of the heavy baskets.

When they had finished, the soldier pulled out his cards, and the playing began again. The soldier won over and over, until by early morning he had collected all of the gold and silver for himself.

The devils were very angry. They were unaccustomed to losing at their favorite game.

"After him!"cried the oldest devil. "Tie his beard into a thousand knots!"

The soldier calmly reached behind him for the old sack the beggar had given him.

"Before you tie my beard into a thousand knots," said the soldier, "tell me, what do you think this is?"

"Anyone can see it's just a dirty old sack!" screamed the oldest devil.

"Is it?" asked the soldier. "Then, by all that's holy, jump into it!"

The devils couldn't help themselves. They jumped into the sack, one after the other, making a terrible racket. When all were safely inside, the soldier quickly tied the sack with heavy twine, hung it on a nail in the wall, and went to sleep for the few hours left of the night.

At dawn, the Tsar sent his servants to the palace to find out what had happened. As they cautiously entered the room, they were surprised to find the soldier happily smoking his pipe, surrounded by baskets and baskets of gold and silver. The soldier told them that now the Tsar and his family could come back to the palace to live.

The devils could be heard screaming angrily from inside the sack, but there was absolutely nothing they could do. The soldier asked the Tsar's servants to bring him a strong horse and wagon in which to carry off his treasure so that he might return to his village and live out his remaining years in comfort. There was so much gold and silver, however, that even the largest wagon the servants could find sagged under its weight.

Last of all, the devils were taken down from the nail and carried outside — still protesting for all they were worth. The villagers surrounded the soldier, congratulating him and praising God for ridding the palace of the pesky devils.

The soldier threw the sack onto the wagon, climbed in, and waved good-bye. The wagon rumbled slowly out of the town and across the countryside until it reached the remotest part of the Bretsky Forest. It would have been a pleasant ride had it not been for the clamor of the devils inside the flour sack. The sun by now was directly over-head, and the soldier felt hungry. He pulled the horse to a stop.

"All right, you old devils," said the soldier, "I am going to put you where I won't be able to hear you, so I can have my lunch in peace!"

And, saying that, the soldier grabbed the heavy flour sack, tied it to his back, and began to climb the tallest tree in the forest. When he reached the topmost branch, he tied the sack to it securely, looked around a few moments at the fine view, and then climbed down to finish his lunch in peace.

Since devils have the highest-pitched and loudest voices of any creature known, lunch wasn't peaceful after all. The soldier didn't know what to do. He was kindhearted enough not to wish the devils undue discomfort, which they would certainly have if he left them hanging forever from that tree branch.

Suddenly he had an idea. He climbed back up to the flour sack, which was swaying in the breeze, and struck up a conversation.

"Old devils," he said, "I have decided to grant you mercy."

"Tell us how so, old soldier," replied the devils.

"I shall release you from this sack if you promise to help me," answered the soldier. "If you trick me, I will call you back into the sack and let you hang here forever."

"Oh, yes, good soldier, let us go and we shall help you in any way!" screamed the delirious devils.

Once again the old soldier tied the sack to his back, this time carefully descending the tall tree to the wagon. Not altogether trusting the devils, he kept them in the sack for the rest of the journey. Of course, he did make sure that they were properly fed and given sips of water.

When the old soldier finally entered his village, everyone came out to greet him. He released the devils from the sack and explained to the villagers that they were his helpers.

Everyone watched in amazement as the devils unloaded all the gold and silver from the wagon. The very next day the soldier took the devils to the best tailor in the village, where he had a fine-looking suit and cap made for each of them.

Now the soldier clearly had more money than he would ever need. He remembered his father and mother telling him that it was selfish for anyone to keep more than he could use for his own wants, and he decided to do something about it. This is what he did.

He put the devils to work around the countryside, searching out the needy and giving enough gold and silver so

that everyone could eat and dress properly and have a good house against the cold Russian winters. At first the devils balked. This wasn't behavior befitting proper devils! But every time they complained, the soldier reminded them of the sack and the tallest tree that waited in the Bretsky Forest.

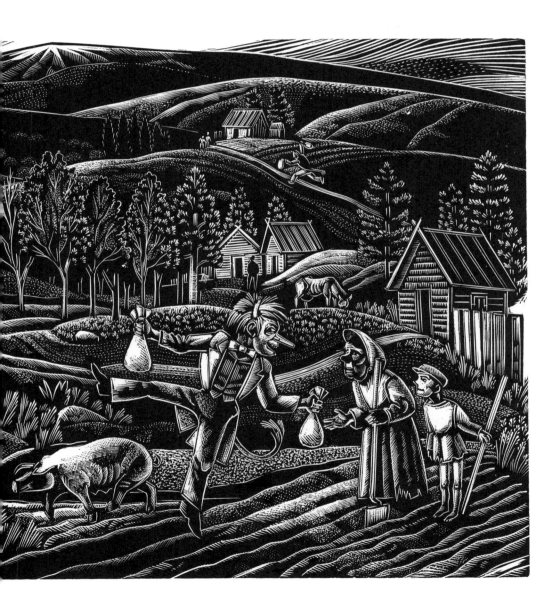

In time, the devils grew quite fond of the old soldier, and rather fond of helping those in need as well. They had plenty to eat themselves, wore fine clothes, and were even occasionally allowed to play their scratchy fiddles and yell to their hearts' content. But only, of course, on a hillside far outside the village, so nobody would be disturbed.